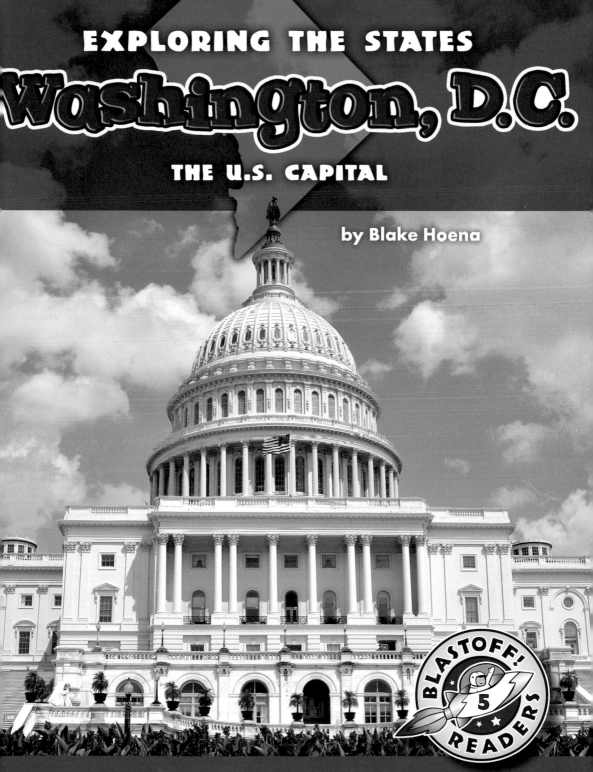

EXPLORING THE STATES

Washington, D.C.

THE U.S. CAPITAL

by Blake Hoena

BELLWETHER MEDIA • MINNEAPOLIS, MN

Note to Librarians, Teachers, and Parents:

Blastoff! Readers are carefully developed by literacy experts and combine standards-based content with developmentally appropriate text.

Level 1 provides the most support through repetition of high-frequency words, light text, predictable sentence patterns, and strong visual support.

Level 2 offers early readers a bit more challenge through varied simple sentences, increased text load, and less repetition of high-frequency words.

Level 3 advances early-fluent readers toward fluency through increased text and concept load, less reliance on visuals, longer sentences, and more literary language.

Level 4 builds reading stamina by providing more text per page, increased use of punctuation, greater variation in sentence patterns, and increasingly challenging vocabulary.

Level 5 encourages children to move from "learning to read" to "reading to learn" by providing even more text, varied writing styles, and less familiar topics.

Whichever book is right for your reader, Blastoff! Readers are the perfect books to build confidence and encourage a love of reading that will last a lifetime!

This edition first published in 2014 by Bellwether Media, Inc.

No part of this publication may be reproduced in whole or in part without written permission of the publisher. For information regarding permission, write to Bellwether Media, Inc., Attention: Permissions Department, 5357 Penn Avenue South, Minneapolis, MN 55419.

Library of Congress Cataloging-in-Publication Data

Hoena, B. A.
 Washington, D.C. / by Blake Hoena.
   pages cm. – (Blastoff! readers. Exploring the states)
 Includes bibliographical references and index.
 Summary: "Developed by literacy experts for students in grades three through seven, this book introduces young readers to the geography and culture of Washington, D.C."– Provided by publisher.
 ISBN 978-1-62617-048-3 (hardcover : alk. paper)
 1. Washington (D.C.)–Juvenile literature. I. Title.
 F194.3.H64 2014
 975.3–dc23
                                                                        2013011516

Printed in the United States of America, North Mankato, MN.

Table of Contents

Where Is Washington, D.C.?

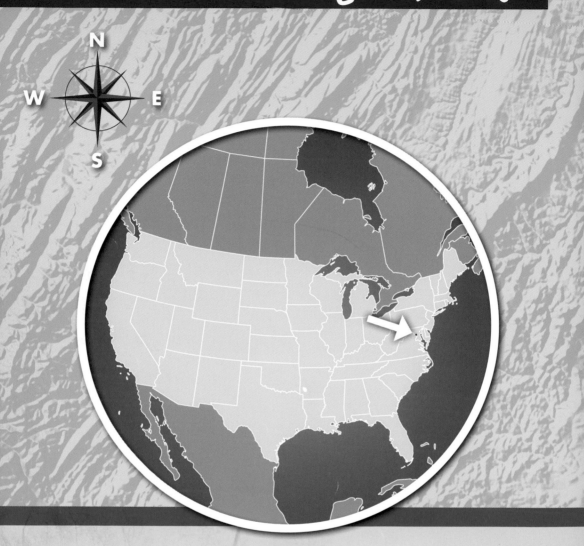

Washington, D.C. is not a state. It is a small **district** that is home to the United States government. The state of Maryland surrounds Washington, D.C. on three sides. The Potomac River forms the district's southwestern border. It separates Washington, D.C. from Virginia.

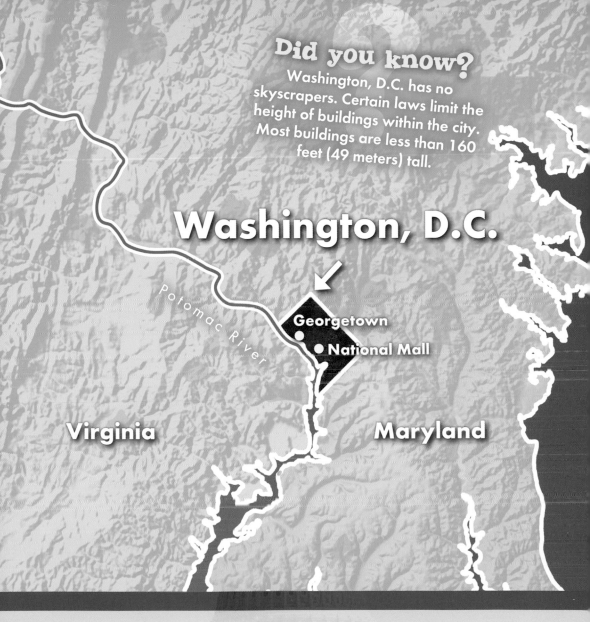

Did you know?
Washington, D.C. has no skyscrapers. Certain laws limit the height of buildings within the city. Most buildings are less than 160 feet (49 meters) tall.

Washington, D.C.

Potomac River

Georgetown

National Mall

Virginia

Maryland

D.C. stands for the District of Columbia. It is named after the explorer Christopher Columbus. While small in size, Washington, D.C. is a big symbol of freedom. It is home to many **monuments** and museums that celebrate our nation's past and present.

The first European explorers sailed up the Potomac River in the early 1600s. They met the Nacotchtank **Native** Americans. Settlers later founded the Maryland **colony**. In 1791, the United States set aside land from both Maryland and Virginia. They later built a capital city for the new country. It is now where government workers from all states gather and make laws.

Did you know?

People in Virginia supported slavery. Washington, D.C. hoped to make slavery illegal. This disagreement caused D.C. to return land to Virginia in 1846.

Washington, D.C. Timeline!

1634: The first colonists arrive in the Maryland colony.

1775-1783: The American colonies fight for independence from Great Britain in the Revolutionary War.

1800: Washington, D.C. becomes the official seat of the U.S. government.

1814: The British burn much of Washington, D.C. during the War of 1812.

1846: The part of Washington, D.C. south of the Potomac River is returned to Virginia.

1865: President Lincoln is shot while attending a play at Ford's Theatre.

1963: Martin Luther King, Jr. delivers his famous "I Have a Dream" speech in front of the Lincoln Memorial.

1964: The people of Washington, D.C. gain the right to vote in presidential elections.

1993: Congress rejects a bill that would make Washington, D.C. a state.

Martin Luther King, Jr.

War of 1812

Ford's Theatre

The Land

The District of Columbia started out as a 100-square-mile (259-square-kilometer) piece of land. It was carved out of Maryland and Virginia, along the Potomac River. This area is a bridge between northern and southern states. When the land was chosen, these parts of the country had divided opinions about **slavery**. Placing the capital city in the middle showed no favor to either side.

Pierre-Charles L'Enfant planned the city. He made the U.S. **Capitol** Building a central part of Washington, D.C. The rest of the city was designed like a grid. The streets running east and west are named with letters of the alphabet. The north-south streets are numbered.

Potomac River

U.S. Capitol Building

Washington, D.C.'s Climate
average °F

spring
Low: 42°
High: 66°

summer
Low: 65°
High: 87°

fall
Low: 46°
High: 69°

winter
Low: 26°
High: 46°

The National Mall

Did you know?

A long reflecting pool stretches between the Lincoln Memorial and the Washington Monument. Its waters reflect the two structures along with the surrounding trees and sky.

Washington Monument

The National Mall is home to many famous museums and historic memorials. The Capitol Building stands on the eastern edge of this long, rectangular park. The Lincoln Memorial overlooks the western end. In the center of the park is the Washington Monument. This marble structure rises 555 feet (169 meters) into the sky.

Several memorials honor soldiers who fought in the nation's wars. Next to the Lincoln Memorial are the Vietnam and Korean War Memorials. The World War II Memorial is one of the Mall's newest monuments. It honors more than 400,000 Americans who died during the war.

Vietnam War Memorial

Lincoln Memorial

Wildlife

Washington, D.C. is a major city. Much of its plant life grows in parks. People enjoy the beautiful white and pink blooms of Japanese cherry trees in the spring. Large oak and willow trees line the streets. Wildflowers such as Virginia bluebells color city parks.

Mostly small animals are found within the district. Raccoons and opossums are common. White-tailed deer and coyotes can also be spotted. Black and gray squirrels scurry up trees in the parks. Wildflowers attract songbirds, while hawks and bald eagles soar above the city.

opossum

Virginia bluebell

Japanese cherry trees

bald eagle

National Air
and Space Museum

The Smithsonian Institution runs several museums along the National Mall. The National Air and Space Museum features historic planes and spacecraft. The Smithsonian American Art Museum exhibits works of art from as early as the 1700s. Items from American culture are on display at the National Museum of American History. Visitors can see the ruby slippers from *The Wizard of Oz* and a piece of Plymouth Rock.

The Washington National Cathedral is one of the area's many historic buildings. The first stone of this magnificent church was laid in 1907. Its central tower rises higher than all other buildings in Washington, D.C.

Washington National Cathedral

fun fact

Many of the stained glass windows in the Washington National Cathedral represent historic events. One window celebrates the first walk on the moon. It even includes a piece of moon rock.

Georgetown

Georgetown was founded in 1751. It belonged to the state of Maryland. In 1791, the community became part of the nation's capital. Georgetown was a major **port** for trading on the Potomac River. It was located at the northernmost point where sea ships could sail up the river.

C&O Canal

Walking through Georgetown today is like traveling through time. Many of the buildings are more than 200 years old. **Tourists** can ride mule-drawn boats down the C&O **Canal**. Actors dress as **colonists** and share stories about colonial life. Visitors can also stop by Georgetown University, the nation's oldest Catholic and **Jesuit** university.

17

Working

Barack Obama
44th President of the United States

The most well-known job in D.C. is President of the United States. However, many other government employees have jobs in Washington. One important agency is the National Aeronautics and Space Administration (NASA). It employs some of the nation's most talented scientists and **engineers**.

Many D.C. workers have **service jobs**. They serve the city's tourists at hotels and restaurants. Some work as tour guides at museums and historic sites. Printing is one of the district's few **manufacturing** activities. Publishers produce all kinds of newspapers, magazines, and books each year.

tour guide

Where People Work in Washington, D.C.

farming and natural resources
1%

services
66%

government
33%

Playing

Washington, D.C. is an **urban** area, but people still enjoy getting outdoors. The city was designed with many parks for residents to stroll through. Boating on the Potomac River is also popular. Theaters and concert halls host plays, ballets, and musical performances.

Sports lovers cheer for the district's professional teams. The Redskins football team has represented D.C. since 1937. Basketball fans root for the Washington Mystics and Wizards. The Nationals baseball team made Washington, D.C. its home in 2005.

fun fact !

The Redskins have won five National Football League Championships, including three Super Bowls.

Mumbo Sauce

Ingredients:

1/2 cup tomato paste

1 cup distilled white vinegar

1 cup pineapple or orange juice

1 cup sugar

4 teaspoons soy sauce

1 teaspoon powdered ginger

1/4 teaspoon hot sauce

Directions:

1. Mix all the ingredients in a pot.

2. Simmer, but do not boil, for about 20 minutes. Add more of any ingredient until it tastes right.

3. Serve warm or at room temperature with fried chicken or french fries.

Ethiopian food

empanadas

People from all over the United States live and work in Washington, D.C. A variety of food is served across the district, including burgers, pizzas, tacos, and seafood. D.C. also caters to many foreign visitors. Foods from around the world are served at its restaurants.

Washington, D.C. is home to the largest Ethiopian population in the United States. People crowd the restaurants of "Little Ethiopia" to share heaping platters of spicy Ethiopian food. The Adams Morgan neighborhood is known for its large Latino population. **Empanadas** are a popular dish served there.

23

Festivals

Washington, D.C. is a city of festivals. At the Smithsonian Folklife Festival, people of every nationality take pride in their culture. They dress in **traditional** clothes and play music from their homelands.

National Cherry Blossom Festival

In 1912, the mayor of Tokyo gave Washington, D.C. 3,000 cherry trees. Every spring, the National Cherry Blossom Festival celebrates this gift as the trees begin to bloom. At Easter, the President's family hosts the White House Easter Egg Roll. Participants use spoons to roll colorful eggs across the White House lawn.

Civil Rights

In August of 1963, Martin Luther King, Jr. led a march through Washington, D.C. At the time, many **minorities** were being treated unfairly. King and other African-American leaders organized the protest to fight for **civil rights**.

More than 200,000 supporters gathered around the Lincoln Memorial as King delivered his famous "I Have a Dream" speech. King's words had a huge impact. Congress later wrote laws to help protect the rights of all people in the United States. This spirit of **activism** makes Washington, D.C. an ongoing symbol of freedom and justice.

The Martin Luther King, Jr. Memorial sits between the Lincoln and Jefferson Memorials. It features famous quotes from King's many speeches about civil rights.

Fast Facts About Washington, D.C.

Washington, D.C.'s Flag

The Washington, D.C. flag has a white background. A row of three five-pointed stars runs across the top of the flag. Below the stars are two red stripes. The design is based on the coat of arms of George Washington's family.

District Nicknames:	D.C.
	The District
District Motto:	*Justitia Omnibus*; "Justice for All"
Founded:	1791
Population:	601,723 (2010)
Area:	68 square miles (176 square kilometers)
Major Industries:	government, tourism
Federal Government:	1 delegate; 0 senators

District Flower
American beauty rose

District Bird
wood thrush

Glossary

activism—the practice of taking action to support a cause

canal—a waterway built to connect larger bodies of water

capitol—the building in which state representatives and senators meet

civil rights—the rights of people to receive equal treatment under the laws of a country

colonists—people who settle new land for their home country

colony—a territory owned and settled by people from another country

district—an area or region

empanadas—pastries that are filled with meat and vegetables and then baked or fried

engineers—workers who use science and math to solve problems or create advanced technology

Jesuit—a member of a Roman Catholic group called the Society of Jesus

manufacturing—a field of work in which people use machines to make products

minorities—groups of people of certain races or ethnicities living among a larger group of people of a different race or ethnicity

monuments—structures that people build to remember important events or people

native—originally from a specific place

port—a place where ships and boats can dock

service jobs—jobs that perform tasks for people or businesses

slavery—a system in which certain people are considered property

tourists—people who travel to visit another place

traditional—relating to a custom, idea, or belief handed down from one generation to the next

urban—relating to cities or city life

To Learn More

AT THE LIBRARY

Jeffrey, Gary. *Martin Luther King Jr. and the March on Washington*. New York, N.Y.: Gareth Stevens, 2013.

Korrell, Emily B. *Awesome Adventures at the Smithsonian: The Official Kids Guide to the Smithsonian Institution*. Washington, D.C.: Smithsonian Books, 2013.

Ollhoff, Jim. *Washington, D.C.* Edina, Minn.: ABDO Publishing, 2010.

ON THE WEB

Learning more about Washington, D.C. is as easy as 1, 2, 3.

1. Go to www.factsurfer.com.

2. Enter "Washington, D.C." into the search box.

3. Click the "Surf" button and you will see a list of related Web sites.

With factsurfer.com, finding more information is just a click away.

Index

The images in this book are reproduced through the courtesy of: Orhan Cam, front cover; SuperStock/ GlowImages, p. 6; (Collection)/ Prints & Photographs Division/ Library of Congress, p. 7 (left); Everett Collection/ SuperStock, p. 7 (middle); trekandshoot, p. 7 (right); S.Borisov, p. 8 (small); Orhan Cam, pp. 8-9; Mayskyphoto, pp. 10-11; Jorg Hackemann, p. 11 (left); Cristina Ciochina, p. 11 (right); artcphotos, p. 12 (top); Mary Terriberry, p. 12 (middle); Songquan Deng, p. 12 (bottom); Chris Humphries, pp. 12-13; kropic1, pp. 14-15; Frances A. Miller, p. 15 (small); Orhan Cam, pp. 16-17; Elan Fleisher/ Look-Foto/ Getty Images, p. 17 (small); Rena Schild, p. 18; Anna Bryukhanova, p. 19; Icon SMI/ Newscom, p. 20; Lissandra Melo, pp. 20-21; The Washington Post/ Getty Images, p. 22; Dereje, p. 23 (small); traveler1116, pp. 24-25; Jeff Malet Photography/ Newscom, p. 25 (small); Francis Miller/ Getty Images, p. 26 (small); hanusst, pp. 26-27; Juan Martinez, p. 28; Chris Hill, p. 29 (left); LanKS, p. 29 (right).